D1306945

DOT JOURNALING

AN INTERACTIVE GUIDE *to* DESIGNING
A CREATIVE & PRACTICAL PLANNER

Written and Illustrated
By Hannah Beilenson

Peter Pauper Press Inc.
WHITE PLAINS, NEW YORK

PETER PAUPER PRESS
Fine Books and Gifts Since 1928

OUR COMPANY

In 1928, at the age of twenty-two, Peter Beilenson began printing books on a small press in the basement of his parents' home in Larchmont, New York. Peter—and later, his wife, Edna—sought to create fine books that sold at "prices even a pauper could afford."

Today, still family owned and operated, Peter Pauper Press continues to honor our founders' legacy—and our customers' expectations—of beauty, quality, and value.

To my parents.
Thanks for letting me do this.

Illustrated by Hannah Beilenson
Additional images used under license from Shutterstock.com
Designed by Heather Zschock

Copyright © 2020
Peter Pauper Press, Inc.
202 Mamaroneck Avenue
White Plains, NY 10601 USA
All rights reserved
ISBN 978-1-4413-3272-1
Printed in China
7 6 5 4 3 2

Visit us at www.peterpauper.com

DOT
Journaling

CONTENTS

INTRODUCTION

How I Came to Dot Journaling

Like a lot of my peers, I started (and restarted, and restarted), journaling through my early tweens and teens. In my first diary, at age 12, I wrote nonstop about my hamster Mapel (yes, spelled "Mapel"), who was always running away. Later, the pages of my journals were filled with first crushes, the trials of middle school, and my ever-changing aspirations (Pop Star! Film Critic! Professional Lipstick Namer!). When I graduated from high school, I had the opportunity to look through some of these journals, and they all had two things in common. 1) that whether I was 11 or 14, I was deeply concerned that I'd find Mapel trapped behind the washing machine, and 2) that the journals were always, at most, only a quarter full. My diaries were not sustainable.

I found dot journaling during college, where, like everyone else, I was trying to do everything at once. I wasn't quite sure what it was, but I saw the concept plastered on YouTube, Pinterest boards, and even BuzzFeed listicles. They were gorgeous—journals that were planners but not, diaries but not—and they were helping tons of people organize their lives. As a student juggling grad school applications, a long-distance relationship, and the flood of final exams, I was willing to try anything to get organized. Three years later, and I'm still dot journaling every day. It might not have fixed my life (not sure if any journal has that power), but it has made me more organized, given me more free time, and, if I say so myself, it is nice to look at.

GETTING STARTED

So...What Is a Dot Journal?

That's a hard question to answer, because a dot journal is whatever you want it to be! It's part scrapbook, part journal, part to-do list, and part planner (and part wish list, part movie guide, part fitness guide, I could go on forever . . .). The dot journal encompasses the best parts of all of these without taking up too much space, and is unique to you. It's perfect to have if you don't want to carry around one million books in your bag!

Okay, But Really, What Is It?

A dot journal is a place for you to record everything crucial (or interesting!) in your day-to-day life! It's for everything you want to remember or need to get done. It's a space for your observations and opinions, to track your exercise habits and guitar playing progress. The journal used is typically a dotted journal, as the evenly spaced marks help make measuring layouts a breeze, but any blank journal will work! The most important thing is that there's room to explore.

But just because there's a good amount of room doesn't necessarily mean it's a lot of writing—remember, this is supposed to make your life easier! So, the things you write down are written concisely to better organize your daily rituals (no Virginia Woolf–length sentences here!). In a dot journal, you can differentiate between tasks and observations, likes and dislikes, through a series of symbols. You can write, "Call with Carol," and depending on the symbol used, you can look back and know whether or not that's a task to be completed, or something that happened that day.

All this is to say that the dot journal should serve your needs! Contrary to popular belief, it doesn't have to be time consuming or perfect! There is, of course, a basic means of organization across the page (which we will go over throughout this book), but this serves both a functional and aesthetic purpose, and can be as intense or as minimalist as you'd like. The dot journal is also organized by dates, page numbers, and an index, so you can always know where you are in your journey, and can easily access any moment.

Does It Work?

Yes, it works. Through dot journaling, I have become more organized, I've found ways to give myself more free time, and am generally less overwhelmed by tasks. But the most meaningful thing this process has provided me—and I hope will provide you as well—is a space where I can map my own growth. I often find that as we reach adulthood, we begin to think of ourselves as static persons. Our bodies aren't changing anymore, and a good amount of "firsts" have passed. It's easy for me to say, "Hi, I'm Hannah, I'm 5'7", have a mild bee allergy, and think the original *Planet of the Apes* movie is the best film ever made." But those things are surface. The growth—the hard stuff—can be difficult to notice. At 23, I'm a better communicator than I was at 19. When I was 18, I couldn't keep my clothes off the floor. Now, I can pack up an apartment in two days. Seeing that growth on paper validates the people we are, while also pushing us toward the people we can become.

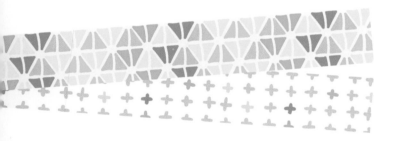

Will It Work for Me?

Yes! Dot journaling is great for everyone! Are you an architect with a passion for bird watching? Congratulations, your dot journal makes space for new building designs, maps out your meetings, and has a tracker for new bird sightings cataloged by region! Are you a stay-at-home parent and a renowned foodie? Great, your dot journal not only organizes your children's after-school activities, but also ranks the best restaurants in your neighborhood by cuisine, plating, and wine selection! Are you a gardener with a flair for ghost hunting? Easy, your dot journal tracks the progress of your favorite seasonal flowers, and has daily sketching space for the strange happenings you see at the abandoned house on Creek Lane.

And if you don't find yourself among these very common examples, dot journaling is also great for people who...

- Like goal setting
- Want to track their habits
- Prefer pen and paper
- Can't journal, but want to
- Want to get organized
- Love to draw and design
- Love to draw and design, but aren't very good at it
- Tend to forget dates
- Like to-do lists
- Have seen dot journals, and wanna know what the hype is all about

This Week

»—— sunday ——→

»—— monday ——→

»—— tuesday ——→

»—— wednesday ——→

»—— thursday ——→

»—— friday ——→

»—— saturday ——→

What Will I Learn?

In this book, you'll learn what a dot journal can be, and examples of popular methods. You'll learn terms and concepts (like logs, trackers, and signifiers), and I'll answer some of the common and not-so-common questions. In every chapter, you'll find multiple examples of the best layouts for whatever approach you want to take (minimalist, detailed, artistic, different by the day!). And with every design you see in this book, you will also have a detailed guide helping you create it. Most importantly, in each chapter, you will be shown how to make your dot journal entirely your own (because just copying is no fun!). In addition to layouts, and tips on how to divide the page, I'll show you practical design techniques that can be worked into any design. Dot journaling is unique, so yours won't look exactly like mine, or anyone else's! But through learning the techniques presented in this book, you can change and make every log, tracker, and collection your own!

BASICS

So, now you know what a dot journal is, but there are a lot of mechanics to consider when moving forward. Future Spread, migration, rapid logging—these are terms you're gonna see pop up again and again. When I first started dot journaling, the hardest part was trying to figure out what everyone was talking about. I had to learn all of these concepts as I went, but I think it's more helpful to have all of the definitions laid out, so if you're ever confused, you can come back here for some quick terminology assistance!

Terms

Dot Journal: An organizational system in a notebook that combines elements of journaling, planning, and tracking to maximize efficiency. This is typically done through utilizing short sentences and rapid logging (so you don't have to spend ten minutes outlining that you have a meeting with your boss on Thursday).

Block: The space between two dots. You'll see this term when I outline how to make different designs on the page.

Rapid Logging: A form of short-form notation. It uses topics and page numbers to organize, and uses bullets and signifiers to differentiate between tasks, events, and observations.

> **Topic:** A short descriptive title at the top of each collection. Each topic should clarify what's happening on the page.
>
> **Bullet:** Mark that indicates the type of event happening. Bullets are divided into tasks, events, and notes.
>
> **Task:** Something you need to do or have done. It is indicated by a dot • and turns into a completed X, migrated >, scheduled <, or canceled /, as needed. A task is also sometimes indicated by a small box □, which can be filled in with the same markings (or different ones, depending on what you prefer).
>
> **Event:** A date-specific entry. It is indicated by an open circle O.
>
> **Note:** An observation, thought, feeling, or thing you want to remember. It is indicated by a dash —.
>
> **Signifier:** A mark you make to the left of a bullet that adds extra context to your task/event. This helps you see quickly what each bullet represents. You can create these as needed, but some common ones are ✱ = priority, $ = shopping, and ! = idea.

Migration: The act of moving events/tasks from one spread/collection to another.

Spreads and Pages: A layout across the page (or multiple pages) defined by time. Spreads can be simple or highly detailed, but their main purpose is to organize part of your dot journal by topic and time frame.

> **Future Spread:** A spread for future/long-term events. While it is commonly divided into 12 or six-month layouts, its purpose is to allow you to mark far-in-advance dates for easy reference.
>
> **Monthly Spread:** A spread focused on the events/tasks of a single month.
>
> **Weekly Spread:** A spread focused on the events/tasks of a single week.
>
> **Daily Spread:** A spread focused on the events/tasks of a single day (sometimes, depending on your preference, there is space for diary entries in this spread).
>
> **Tracker:** A spread where you enter anything you want to keep track of. Often, these spreads are related to fitness, hobbies, mental health, etc., but they can be used for anything you're interested in monitoring (like if you want to see how many hours a week you watch Netflix—no judgment!).

Collection: A group of related ideas on the page organized by topic, and not (necessarily) by time frame.

> **List:** A record of anything you're interested in (movies you'd like to watch, songs you enjoy, shopping staples...)
>
> **Notes:** Thoughts, observations, diary entries
>
> **Mind map:** A collection of loosely organized thoughts/goals/feelings that can move across the page organically. (This concept was popularized by the late British psychology author Tony Buzan.)

More on Migration and Symbols

Looking at some of the definitions I've given you, you've probably noticed the term migration and the concept of changing dots to circles to slashes, and thought, What? How am I supposed to move and change things once they've already been written down?

While the dot journal isn't a computer, there is still a lot of room for movement! **Migration is the act of moving tasks/events from one spread/collection to another.** Often, we might plan a task for one day and find we don't have time for it, or an event scheduled is suddenly rescheduled, or you thought you would have to do the dishes but your roommate already did that (oh, to be blessed with good roommates), and when these things happen, there are clean and easy ways to mark those changes, so you can look at your journal, and be confident in what you need to do and what you don't.

So, how do we do this? **Typically, everything starts with a dot, and that dot is changed depending on how the task plays out.** Here are some variations on an example:

- Say you have to clean your apartment—this would begin as a dot •. You clean your apartment, and change that dot to an X.

- Say you have to clean your apartment sometime this week, and schedule it for Wednesday. You would change the dot to a "less than" symbol <.

- Say you have to clean your apartment, but it just doesn't happen. This is where migration comes in. You can change the dot to a "greater than" symbol >, and move the task to a new day/week/month.

This makes it clear at a glance what tasks still need doing, which you've finished, and which have been moved!

Key

All these symbols can be a lot to keep track of, especially since you might be making a bunch of them up yourself. Symbols are always going to be specific to your life, so it's good to have a place to monitor them, especially since the symbols you use might change over time. This is why the **Key**—your list of all your symbols—is so useful! It also allows you to further individualize how you categorize. Since events are open circles, I love to color them in depending on if they're work events, date nights, or household work. You can put your Key anywhere, but I usually put the Key on the first page of my journal so I have it right by the Index (see next page).

KEY

•	Task	▨	Work
<	Task in Progress	▨	School
X	Task Complete	■	Family
>	Task Migrated	■	Social
/	Task Cancelled	▨	Chores
o	Event	▨	Misc.
-	Note		
◖	Watch		
♡	Inspiration		

DIMENSIONS

Across - 26 blocks (half - 13)

Down - 39 blocks (half - 19.5)

Index

The **Index** will help you keep track of where things appear in your dot journal. Maybe you want to know how your mood was during the month of February. Your Index will tell you the page of your Mood Tracker for that month. Yes, this means you need to number your dot journal pages. Yes, it's mandatory. (Believe me: Six months from now when you want to find a collection about your Best Worst Movies in a pinch, you will thank me.)

Essentially, each time you create a new spread or collection, you will name that collection and the corresponding page number in your Index. In the beginning, there won't be much to put here, aside from your Future Log, but as you continue, you'll be surprised at how quickly the Index fills up, so I recommend giving yourself at least two pages for it, or organize your Index into two columns.

Now, not everything needs to go into your Index, as it might be time consuming to include every daily entry. But I think it's good practice to include each monthly spread, each tracker, and each new collection. That way, when someone asks you to show them one of your dot journal layouts, you can quickly find your coolest calendar spread and show them what's up.

You can also organize your Index by topic. So, every entry that pertains to the home can just be titled home, with each page it's mentioned being marked (think things like food shopping, chores, school schedules, date ideas, etc.). But again, how you organize is up to you! I've included a few examples so you can see how I like to set it up with minimal effort.

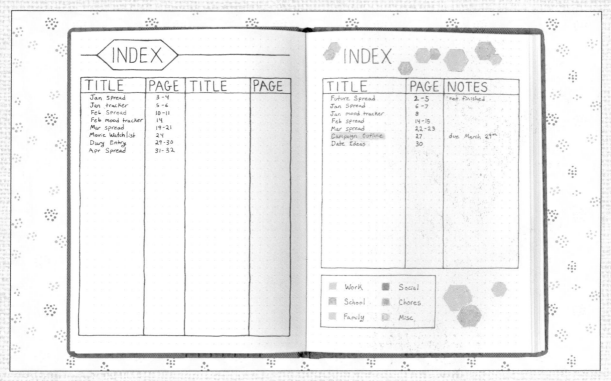

INDEX

TITLE	PAGE	TITLE	PAGE
Jan Spread	3-4		
Jan tracker	5-6		
Feb Spread	10-11		
Feb mood tracker	14		
Mar spread	19-21		
Movie Watchlist	24		
Diary Entry	29-30		
Apr Spread	31-32		

INDEX

TITLE	PAGE	NOTES
Future Spread	2-5	not finished
Jan Spread	6-7	
Jan mood tracker	8	
Feb spread	14-15	
Mar spread	22-23	
Campaign Outline	27	due March 29th
Date Ideas	30	

- ☐ Work
- ☐ School
- ☐ Family
- ☐ Social
- ☐ Chores
- ☐ Misc

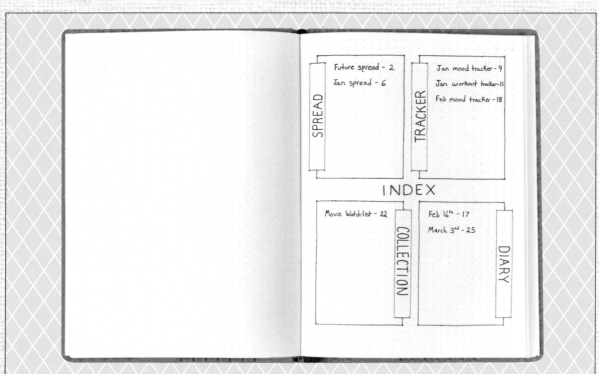

INDEX

SPREAD
- Future spread - 2
- Jan spread - 6

TRACKER
- Jan mood tracker - 9
- Jan workout tracker - 11
- Feb mood tracker - 18

COLLECTION
- Movie Watchlist - 22

DIARY
- Feb 16th - 17
- March 3rd - 25

A helpful tip:

I think this is a good time to mention that yes, you will add new pages at strange times. You're halfway through March and want to add a Gratitude Log? Great! You want to give yourself sketch pages even though it's only Tuesday? Perfect! Your Dot Journal is meant to support your life and the way it changes, so don't try to constrict when new collections/spreads can appear. It's a lot more fun if you let things happen naturally, and mark them in your Index accordingly.

Putting It All Together

- Dot journaling is meant to help you organize. This is done through the creation of spreads, collections, rapid logging, and migration.
- At the end of each day/week/month, check your spread for unfinished tasks, and migrate them to the next spread.
- Keep track of your symbols using a Key.
- Each time you create a new spread/collection, add it to your Index.

essentials

DOT MATRIX NOTEBOOK

- For bullet journaling, graphs, charts, designs, drawings, notes, and more
- A4 Notebook size (8¼ in. x 11¾ in.)
- 192 dot-grid pages
- Elastic band closure
- Ribbon bookmark
- Acid-free/archival paper
- Binding lies flat for ease of use.
- Inside back cover pocket

always create
never compromise

Necessary Tools

There are a few tools you need to really get started. It's the worst when you're working on a spread, and realize that you don't have the right pen or ruler! So here are a few (in my opinion) necessary items to get started:

Notebook: Listen, you can technically use any notebook for dot journaling (blank, lined, gridded, etc.), but "dot" is in the name "dot journaling" for a reason! I personally recommend using a dotted journal because it makes creating clean spreads a breeze, without overwhelming the eye. Dot journals allow you to sketch without getting distracted by the marks on the page. You're also going to want a journal that's large enough for your spreads/

collections, without being too large for your backpack. The standard size is an A5 notebook (5-3/4" wide × 8-1/4" high, or 14.8 cm wide × 21 cm high). Try to find something with thick pages to avoid bleed-through (thank goodness for Amazon.com reviews) and something that feels sturdy when you hold it.

Pencils: If you want to avoid unnecessary pain, I recommend always starting your spreads in pencil. Nothing drives me mad like an uneven box because I was rushing to finish a spread.

STUDIO SERIES™	B
STUDIO SERIES™	2B
STUDIO SERIES™	3B
STUDIO SERIES™	4B
STUDIO SERIES™	5B
STUDIO SERIES™	6B
STUDIO SERIES™	8B

Fine liners: Fine liners are plastic-tipped pens that work well for writing, drawing, and sketching. You can use a ballpoint pen for dot journaling, but fine liners tend to have less bleed-through, and come in more colors!

Ruler: A good, small ruler that fits in the back pocket of your dot journal is a godsend. These help you make clean, even lines, and can bring your dot journaling from "finger painter" to "Renaissance artist" with the stroke of a pen.

Correction fluid or tape: You're going to make mistakes. Even if you take every precaution, even if you take three hours to do each spread (which I do not recommend), you will make mistakes. Try not to beat yourself up over it. Whichever product you use is your preference, and a little here and there will protect your spreads from even the most eagle-eyed critic.

If you want to get really crazy, here are some optional tools that can bring your spreads and collections to the next level. NOTE: these are not necessary, and you can still create a Pinterest-worthy dot journal without them. But if you're anything like me—meaning you can spend four hours in a Michael's—these tools are fun to keep in the back of your mind:

Brush pens: Brush pens bring watercolor effects to dot journaling with ease. They're great if you want to add a little calligraphy to the page.

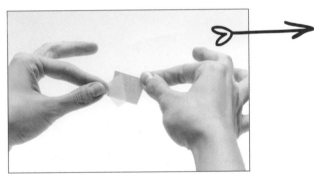

Double-sided tape: Double-sided tape allows you to layer pages/designs in your spreads. It's especially great if you come from a scrapbooking background.

Stencils: Stencils are excellent for decreasing design time. I find simple shapes particularly useful, especially if you repeat spread designs in your dot journal. Just make sure that they're aligned to the dot distance in your notebook.

Stamps: Stamps are a quick way to add some fun decals to your dot journal. I love to use them next to titles, or if there's any blank space on the page I want to fill.

Washi tape: Washi tape is a Japanese paper masking tape that you can use to add color and patterns to your spreads with ease.

Highlighters: Highlighters can add a little flair to your tasks/events. Anything you really want to remember, you can highlight! It's not only a reminder, it also brightens up the page.

Studio Series Gel Highlighters: Uniquely formulated waxy highlighters in six neon colors: yellow, orange, green, blue, purple, and pink.

Page markers: Not just for reference books or documents, "sticky" page markers can be used to mark any page you need to find, without damaging your artwork or the paper. If there's a particular spread or collection you return to often, and don't want to keep checking your Index, page markers make for a strong alternative.

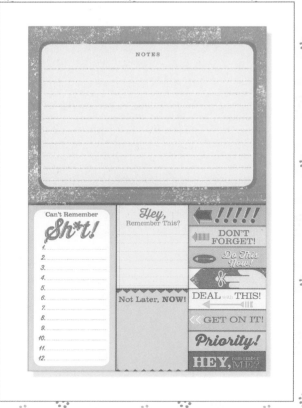

Sticky notes: I really like to use plain or decorative sticky notes for repeating/changing spreads. If you want to use the same grocery list spread (instead of remaking it each month), sticky notes can be used to give designs a little more flexibility.

FUTURE SPREADS

Think of the Future Spread as your calendar for the year, like the ones hanging in your aunt's living room with shirtless firemen (that's a universal experience, right?). It's a place to mark events far in the future that you don't want to forget—birthdays, yearly doctor's appointments, etc. (for me, it's when to renew my parking permit so I don't get stuck in the back lot). These spreads can be expansive, taking up multiple pages, or they can fit snugly on one page—though to make the one page spread work, you're going to want to make use of the symbols we went over in the last chapter. Remember—don't feel like you must fill in the Future Spread with every single task and event, as you're still going to have Monthly, Weekly, and Daily Spreads for the day-to-day.

Do I Have to Wait Until January to Start My Journal?

Absolutely not! Imagine discovering dot journaling on February 1st, only to learn that you'd have to wait 11 months to start. As an instructor, and a student, my year starts in late August, so I like to begin my dot journal then as well. You should start whenever you want to! I realize there's the temptation to make everything perfectly neat and even, but it's important to remember that this method is meant to serve you, not the Gregorian calendar.

Does the Spread Have to Be 12 Months?

No, but I usually find it easier when it's a full year. Consider the following situation: Someone gifts you a woodworking class five months in advance, but your Future Spread only goes forward four months. It doesn't take much work to make the spread fit a year, and it will save you the hassle later. That being said, this is your journal, so feel free to do what suits you best, and all of the templates can be easily modified to serve less-than-12-month calendars.

FUTURE SPREAD 1: DATES AND EVENTS

This layout is perfect if you don't want your Future Spread to take up a ton of space in your journal. The mini calendars on the left side let you know what dates fall on which day of the week, while the right page leaves plenty of room to put upcoming appointments, birthdays, and deadlines. The block-heavy design is clean, sharp, and best of all, super easy to do.

What you need: A pencil, a ruler

Optional: Square stencil for months on the "Events" page (this can totally be done with just a ruler though!)

Color scheme: Black for outline, blue for winter months, pink for spring months, orange for summer months, red for fall months

ng Forward -2020

January

S	M	T	W	T	F	S
			1	2	3	4
5	6	7	8	9	10	11
12	13	14	15	16	17	18
19	20	21	22	23	24	25
26	27	28	29	30	31	

April

S	M	T	W	T	F	S
			1	2	3	4
5	6	7	8	9	10	11
12	13	14	15	16	17	18
19	20	21	22	23	24	25
26	27	28	29	30		

May

S	M	T	W	T	F	S
					1	2
3	4	5	6	7	8	9
10	11	12	13	14	15	16
17	18	19	20	21	22	23
24	25	26	27	28	29	30
31						

March

S	M	T	W	T	F	S
1	2	3	4	5	6	7
8	9	10	11	12	13	14
15	16	17	18	19	20	21
22	23	24	25	26	27	28
29	30	31				

June

S	M	T	W	T	F	S
	1	2	3	4	5	6
7	8	9	10	11	12	13
14	15	16	17	18	19	20
21	22	23	24	25	26	27
28	29	30				

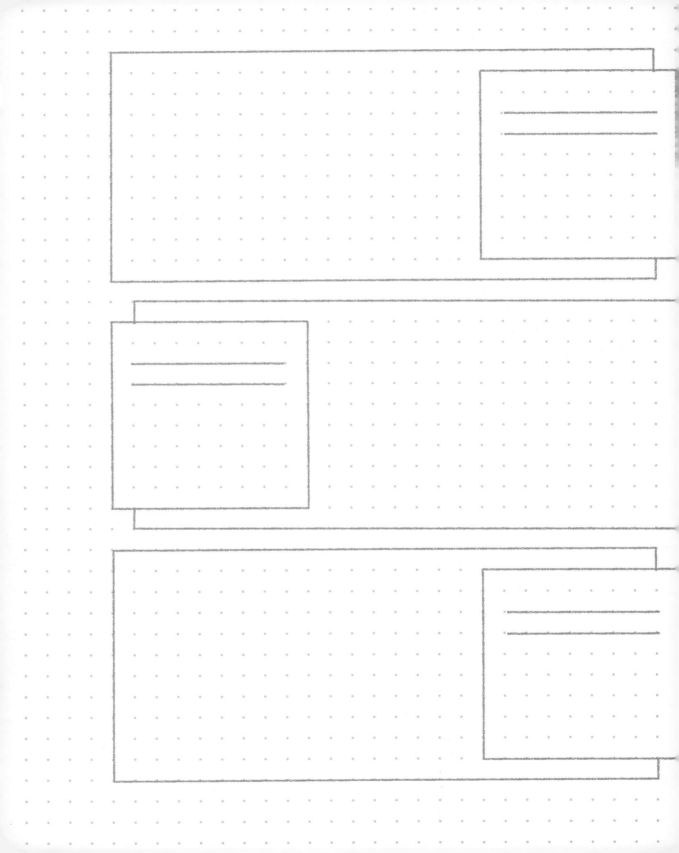

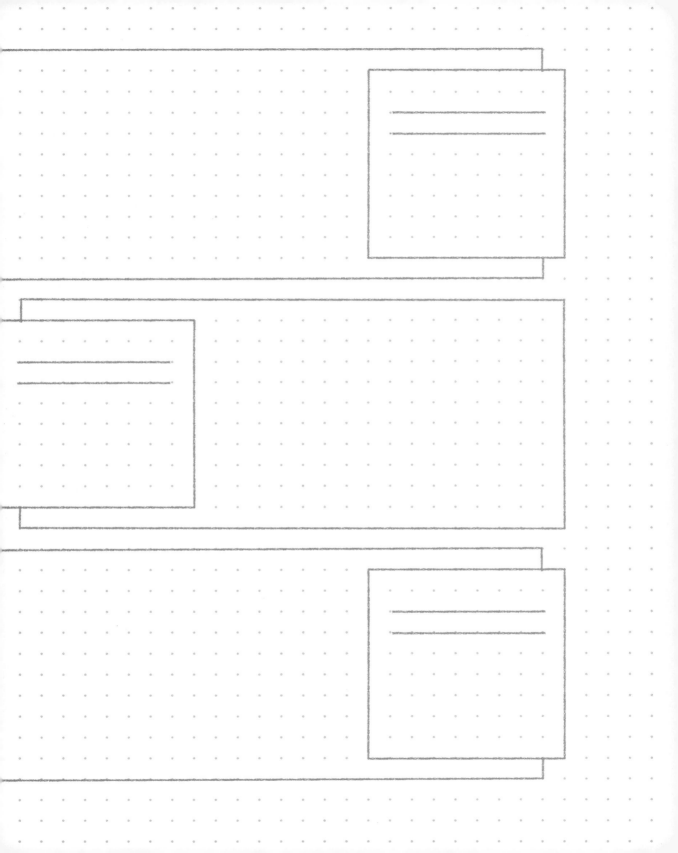

FUTURE SPREAD 3: VERTICAL

I'm always amazed by this spread, because it does so much with so little. It features four months per page, and the length of the boxes varies depending on the amount of days in the month, which adds a good bit of flair to this design. This spread essentially depends on one large box that is then split up into columns, so it's very easy to do, but be warned, there's less room to write out events, so be ready to use rapid logging symbols and some color coding if you want to attempt it.

What you need: A pencil, a ruler
Optional: Stencil for title lettering (I used Peter Pauper Press's Essentials Dotted Journal Stencil Set.)
Color scheme: Black outline, light blue for title

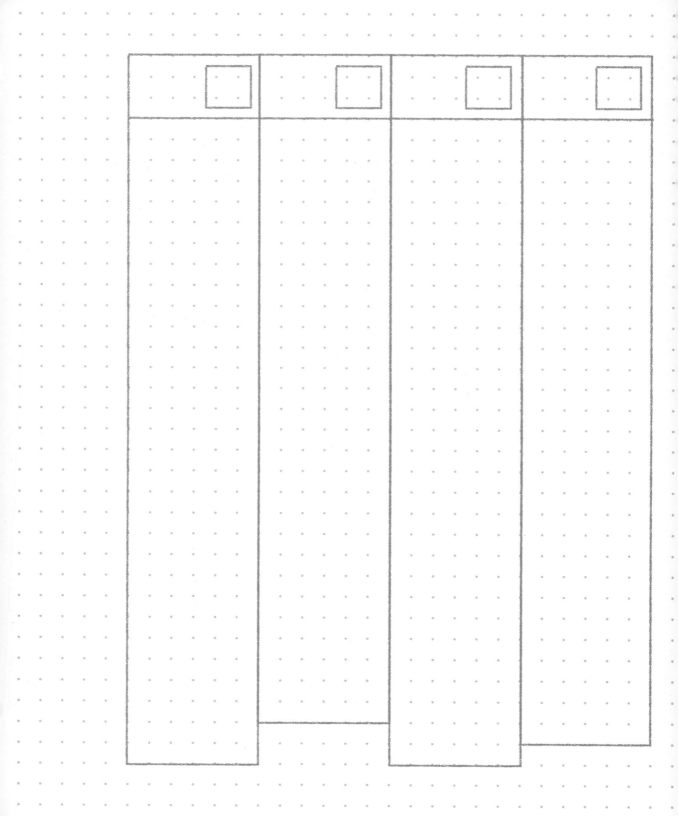

FUTURE SPREAD 4: ADVANCED

I'm obsessed with this spread, and not just because it reminds me of 1990s cartoon logos. The smooth edges, coupled with the silly lettering, is so pleasing, and a lot of fun to make. This spread features six months per page, with alternating headings to keep things interesting. I shouldn't even be calling it "advanced," because it's not all that hard to do, just a little more time consuming. Rounding out the edges of your boxes takes some patience, and you're going to want to be careful when placing your stencils. Go slow, start in pencil, and you're golden.

What you need: A pencil, a ruler, small oval stencil
Color scheme: Light blue for months, pale purple for month fill/title fill, dark purple for all outlines

A helpful tip: If you want to do this lettering, try making bubble letters fast and loose. The imperfections are going to work in your favor—when the words fall in line, it'll look totally purposeful and fun.

AT LARGE

Jan

Mar

May

Jul

Aug

Sep

Oct

Nov

Dec

MONTHLY SPREADS

After you finish your Future Spread, you're going to want to focus on a Monthly Spread. I find it helpful to think of dot journaling as a means of narrowing down, of moving from bird's-eye to magnifying view. The Monthly Spread is a space for you to outline big events and tasks for a single month—you don't need to put your day-to-day lists here, but you want to be able to map out the arc the next 30 days might take.

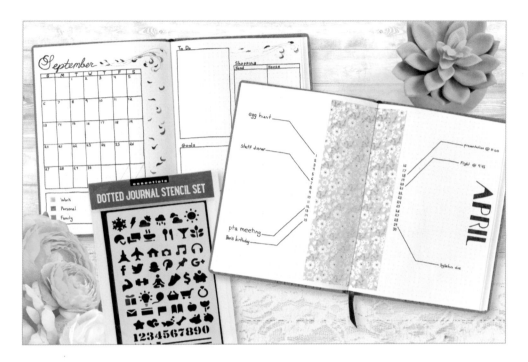

How simple or detailed your Monthly Spread is, is entirely up to you. While some just like to put in a basic calendar to mark birthdays, due dates, and tasks, others like to expand their spreads to include things like goals, gratitudes, and gift ideas. You might want to write "finish group project by the end of month" or "application deadline—March 5." How detailed you get here depends on what tracking system works best for you.

Unlike the Future Spread, which you make for the entire upcoming year, you're going to make the Monthly Spreads as they come. You don't need to make each spread months in advance, as you want the dot journal to be able to change and grow with you. The designs you'll want to use, the things you'll want to track, even the way you write, will change as time goes on. So, if it's June, just make the spread for that month, and at the end of June, you can make the July layout and migrate your tasks over to the new spread when you do so.

MONTHLY SPREAD 1: LISTS AND BLOCKS

This spread is great if you: a) don't love drawing calendars, b) have a lot of tasks/events to keep track of, and/or c) like having a lot of room for extra design elements. This spread goes across two pages, with the first page featuring a split column to allow you to designate events as associated with either "work" or "home." On the second page, boxes allocated to "notes," "goals," and "tasks" allow you to further expand on any important dates, and provide space for you to mark any overarching themes for the month and anything else you want to keep track of.

What you need: A pencil, a ruler
Color scheme: Black for outline and title, dark green for subtitles, various shades of green and brown for succulents, various shades of brown for pots.

A helpful tip: Succulents are an excellent design to use when first starting out, because they're all basically just strange shapes in pots. For sweet, simple designs, try sticking to monochromatic color schemes (or, don't get too caught up trying to shade everything). If you find yourself hitting a wall, google "succulent doodles," and you'll have plenty of great base designs at your disposal.

August   Keep in mind...

HOME

NOTES

GOALS

TASKS

AUG

S	M	T	W	T	F	S
						1
2	3	4	5	6	7	8
9	10	11	12	13	14	15
16	17	18	19	20	21	22
23	24	25	26	27	28	29
30	31					

- ☐ Work
- ☐ School
- ☐ Family
- ☐ Social
- ☐ Chores
- ☐ Misc.

MONTHLY SPREAD 2: SPLIT CALENDAR

If you like having a full calendar to look at, but also want access to some space to write, this spread is perfect for you. Since it has a full calendar on the left page, you can easily mark birthdays, dinners, and due dates, but if you need to expand on any important dates, you have the whole right page to put any extra information you feel is important. In this example, I put a few basic things someone might want to keep track of (to-do list, goals, savings tracker, shopping list, etc.), but you should put whatever fits best with your day-to-day life!

What you need: A pencil, a ruler
Color scheme: Black for outline, deep red for title and subtitles, varying shades of brown and orange for the leaves, gray for the wind

A helpful tip: Windblown leaves are another super intuitive design to use in your dot journal. All you need to do is draw swirls for the wind, and make the leaves follow them. The leaves don't even have to be detailed—I myself just drew little crescents. You'll find that context does a lot of work for you, so quick designs create elegant, quickly understood spreads.

Halloween party

grant proposal due

Dinner w/mom

OCTOBER
26 27 28 29 30 31 1 2 3 4 5 6 7 8 9 10 11 12 13 14 15 16 17 18 19 20 21 22 23 24 25

Mark's birthday

potluck

conference call w/editor

movie-night w/ Jill

MONTHLY SPREAD 4: WASHI DESIGN

It almost isn't fair, for something so simple to look so good. Like the Circular Calendar, if you only need to mark dates, this is a great spread to use. It's also incredibly easy to set up (I'm talking less than ten minutes), and looks so much more complicated than it actually is. There's really no way to lose with this design. In the center of the page there are strips of washi tape (or if you'd prefer, you can draw your own design here) which branch out into any important upcoming dates. Seriously, that's it.

What you need: A pencil, a ruler
Optional: Washi tape
Color scheme: Dark green for title and dates, black for branches

egg h

staff din

pta meetin

Ben's birthday

A helpful tip: If you decide against using washi tape, you can totally make your own design! Just mark out the borders using a ruler and pencil, and fill in with whatever illustration you'd like.

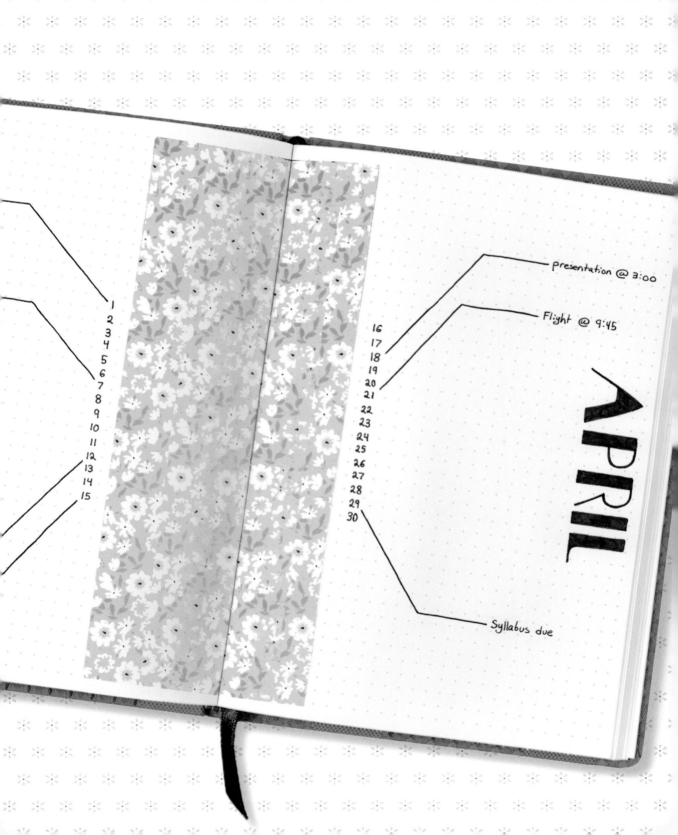

1
2
3
4
5
6
7
8
9
10
11
12
13
14
15

16
17
18
19
20
21
22
23
24
25
26
27
28
29
30

Presentation @ 3:00

Flight @ 9:45

APRIL

Syllabus due

WEEKLY SPREADS

The Weekly Spread is where most of us do the bulk of our dot journaling. It offers space not just to focus on the overarching tasks of the week, but also space for specific day-to-day tasks and activities. This is why many find that their Weekly Spreads occupy the most real estate in their journals (this is especially the case if you're not very interested in having your dot journal function as a diary). For some, the Weekly Spread works for big picture stuff, but doesn't leave enough room for things like daily observations, passing thoughts, or new ideas. This is why the Daily Spread can complement the Weekly so well.

However, don't feel like you must write down everything if you don't want to—plenty of people just use Weekly Spreads and love them. If you choose to only focus on this spread, you'll find yourself with a lot less work. Instead of creating a new layout every day, you only have to set one up at the beginning of each week, and then fill in as you go.

WEEKLY SPREAD 1: BY THE HOUR

If you're looking for a weekly spread that does everything, this is the one for you. It fits two days per page, and each task and event can be marked on the hour, so you not only know what you need to do, but also when you need to do it. Along the bottom of the page, you can keep track of what you eat, and at the top right corner, there's room for you to take note of the weather. In my example, I used doodles to indicate the weather, but you can also just use this space to write the temperature.

What you need: A pencil, a ruler
Color scheme: Black for outline, pale blue for weather background, gray for clouds, yellow for sun, dark blue for rain

...day
Feb 2

Tuesday
Feb 3

| 7 |
| 8 |
| 9 |
| 10 |
| 11 |
| 12 |
| 1 |
| 2 |
| 3 |
| 4 |
| 5 |
| 6 |
| 7 |
| 8 |
| 9 |
| 10 |
| 11 |

Breakfast

Lunch

Dinner

Wednesday
Feb 4

Thursday
Feb 5

| 7 |
| 8 |
| 9 |
| 10 |
| 11 |
| 12 |
| 1 |
| 2 |
| 3 |
| 4 |
| 5 |
| 6 |
| 7 |
| 8 |
| 9 |
| 10 |
| 11 |

Breakfast

Lunch

Dinner

| 7 |
| 8 |
| 9 |
| 10 |
| 11 |
| 12 |
| 1 |
| 2 |
| 3 |
| 4 |
| 5 |
| 6 |
| 7 |
| 8 |
| 9 |
| 10 |
| 11 |

Breakfast

Lunch

Dinner

WEEKLY SPREAD 2: SINGLE PAGE TO-DO

This spread is great if you're looking to save pages in your journal while still having enough room to write down everything going on in the upcoming week. On one half of the page, the dates of the week are outlined with space for events, while the right side offers space to mark tasks that need to get done. It also features two extra boxes at the bottom, which I used for a dinner menu and notes for the next week, but you can change up how the boxes are used depending on what you want to keep track of during the week. It's both simple and versatile.

What you need:
A pencil, a ruler
Color scheme:
Black for outline and title, gold for box accents and week highlight

WEEKLY SPREAD 3: TWO-PAGE TRACKER

If you're anything like me, there's always something around the house that needs doing but never gets done. Having those things noted on my weekly pages is really helpful for me. This spread on the left page offers tons of space to put the day-to-day tasks and events for the upcoming week, while the right page offers two trackers, as well as a notes box. Each tracker can be colored in or marked with an "X" when the task is completed, and believe me, the satisfaction that comes with filling in the boxes is so good.

What you need: A pencil, a ruler
Color scheme: Black for outline and titles, blue for fill-in

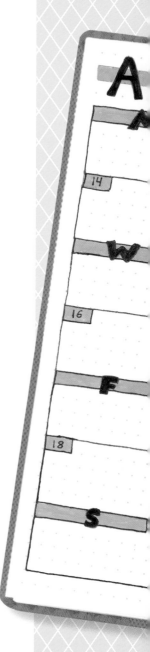

A helpful tip: In this example, there are only two trackers, one for chores, and one for wellness, so to better fill the page, each task is actually two blocks across and two blocks up. If you want, you can give yourself room on the page for up to four trackers, by giving each task only a single block.

IL

WEEK 3

13

T

15

T

17

S

19

CHORES

Grocery shopping
Laundry
Dishes
Bed-sheets
Bathroom Clean

M	T	W	T	F	S	S

WELLNESS

Yoga
Water - 8 glasses
Healthy dinner
Therapy
Medications

M	T	W	T	F	S	S

NOTES

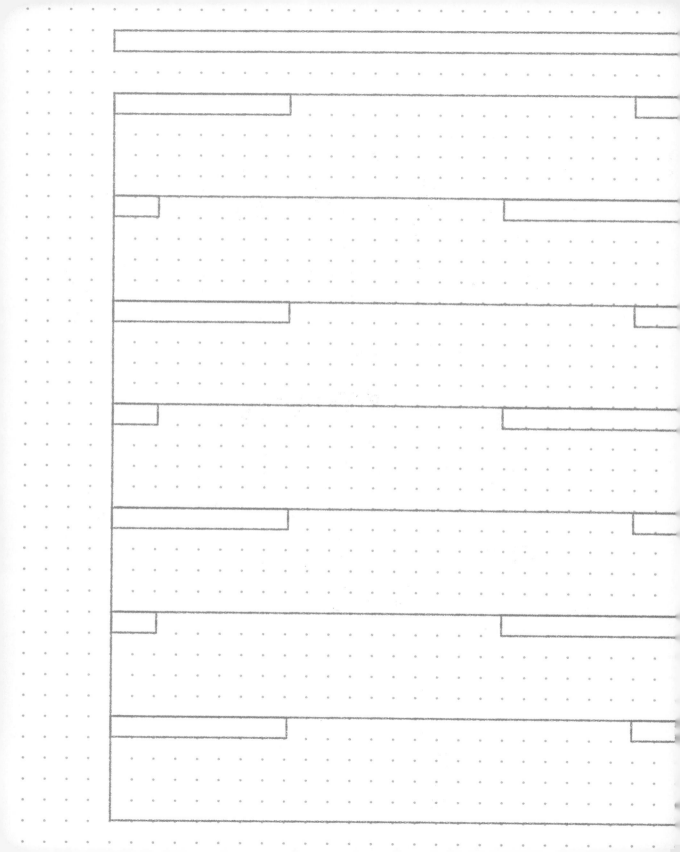

WEEKLY SPREAD 4: TRAPEZOIDS

I consider this spread to be easy, effective, and eye-catching. Like one of the earlier spreads, this one is also a single page, but it really prioritizes look over function. Don't get me wrong, it's still enough room to mark tasks and events for the week, but it won't have extra room for things like menus, note boxes, or trackers. This is a minimalist spread, even if it doesn't look it. And the best part of it being a minimalist spread, is that it's surprisingly easy to make. The trapezoids add a lot of flair, but the layout is essentially boxes split diagonally. If you're short on time, but looking for a spread you can show off, this one is on the money.

What you need: A pencil, a ruler
Color scheme: Black for outline, pink and maroon for title, maroon for dates/days of the week

A helpful tip: I know I always say start in pencil, but for this spread it's absolutely crucial. Instead of trying to draw the trapezoids, just make boxes, draw the diagonal lines on top, and erase what's in-between.

DAILY SPREADS

The Daily Spread, in my opinion, is one of the most fun! You'll spend a lot of time with these pages, and not just because there are 365 days a year (as opposed to 12 months and 52 weeks— wow the Daily Spread sure does take up a lot of real estate). You'll spend a lot of time with the Daily Spread because ultimately, it gets sh*t done.

As I said in the last chapter, not everyone feels the need to use dailies all the time, or at all, but if you do, you'll often find yourself surprised and impressed by how it can increase your productivity. The Daily Spread forces you to take stock of what needs to get done every morning (or every night—looking at you, Night Owls), and having it written down really does help it get done. Go forth and be productive.

Can I Use Dailies as a Diary?

Part of what I loved most about journaling as a kid was having the space to talk about all the weird wonderful stuff that happened that day, and part of the joy now is being able to look back at that writing and see how I thought of, and responded to things when I was younger. I'd hate to be deprived of that now, which is why I'm so glad there's tons of room within dot journaling for traditional diary entries.

You have a few different options for including a diary in your dot journal. The first, and easiest, is just to incorporate it into your Daily Spread. If you use the first Spread, just add a dash (—) and write away. Some of the other pages also include spots for observations, feelings, and memories, so if you want a diary aspect, but don't want to write paragraphs about your day, it's a great middle ground.

SOME IDEAS FOR DIARY ENTRIES:

Gratitudes. Spend some time writing about something that you're grateful for each day.

Strange observations. There's a detective in all of us, but these are great for taking a moment, and really observing the world around you.

Today I felt . . . I like to use these for checking in with myself, emotionally. Knowing how I feel keeps me making smart decisions, and lets me know if I should reach out for support.

DAILY SPREAD 1: SIMPLE AND EASY

Because this layout is so easy, I've included four more complex alternatives, but this is actually the page I use for my dailies, so it's the real deal. Bottom line, this layout is flexible. If you want to spend three pages on a single day, you can. If you only have one thing to get done, then the amount of space on the page used reflects that. And, as it bears repeating, it's great for diary entries. There's no limit to how much you can write, but the lines still leave the page looking clean. This is an excellent option if you don't want to spend a lot of time making a Daily Spread (especially if you plan on using one every single day).

What you need: A pencil, a ruler
Color scheme: Black for outline, coral for flags

nday

DAILY SPREAD 2: TASKS BY HOUR

If I had a dollar for each time I procrastinated on one project by working on a different one, I'd be able to pay my roommate back for her coffee that I drank on 15 different all-nighters. Admittedly, it can be a little overwhelming to have a bunch of tasks lumped together, especially if they all have to get done at different times. This page alleviates that stress by splitting tasks and events into "Morning," "Afternoon," and "Evening" sections. These sections not only help you visualize your day, but they also make sure that you get things done in the order they need to be finished. There's also space for chores and purchases, to make sure that your living space and your wallet aren't victims of your busy schedule 😊.

What you need: A pencil, a ruler
Color scheme: Black for boxes and shadows, yellow for subtitles, yellow and blue for header

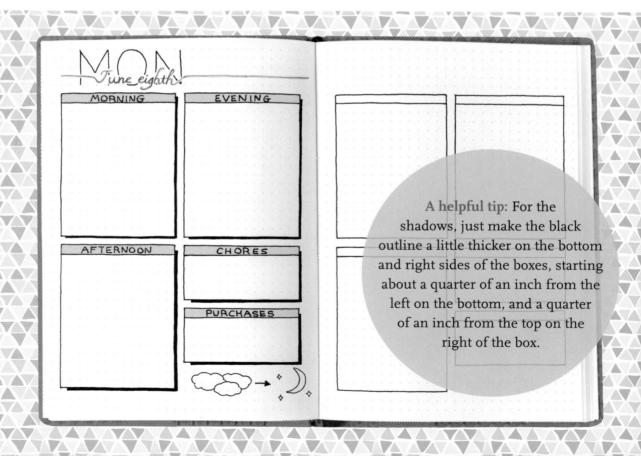

A helpful tip: For the shadows, just make the black outline a little thicker on the bottom and right sides of the boxes, starting about a quarter of an inch from the left on the bottom, and a quarter of an inch from the top on the right of the box.

WED

TASKS

REMEMBER

MOOD

SLEEP
ZZZZZZZZ

WATER
○○○○○○○

GRATITUDES

EVENTS

NAH-TITUDES

NOTES

DAILY SPREAD 3: DAILY TRACKING

Sometimes, it's not only about what needs to get done, but what you're doing to take care of yourself. This layout makes room for simple trackers that allow you to assess your daily habits, as well as room for you to mark events, tasks, notes, reminders, and more (proof that a page, with enough boxes, really can fit everything!). Part of what makes this Daily so successful is that it's split considering how much you actually have to do on a single day. Most people don't have 20 or 30 tasks per day, so with that in mind, this page is organized on the assumption that there are other things that deserved space to be recorded, including mood level, sleep, and water intake.

What you need: A pencil, a ruler
Color scheme: Black for boxes and trackers, green for subtitles, aqua and green for header

DAILY SPREAD 4: MOOD-FOCUSED

If you find that your Weekly Spread outlines your tasks reliably, then you should use a Daily Spread that prioritizes other aspects of your life. This mood-focused layout builds upon what the daily tracking layout does in a big way. By removing tasks and events entirely from the equation, there's room to turn an eye inward and focus on the self. There's not only space for you to write down your highs and lows of the day, but also space for some daily writing, productivity/energy/confidence trackers, and a beautiful mood wheel. I find this page especially useful if you're looking to keep an eye on your mental health and want a physical means to see your own growth over time.

What you need: A pencil, a ruler, small circular stencil for productivity/energy/confidence tracker, protractor, and stencils for mood wheel 1-¾" (45 mm) circular stencil, 2-¼" (57 mm) circular stencil, 2-¾" (70 mm) circular stencil
Color scheme: Black for boxes, header, subtitles, pale purple for productivity/energy/ confidence trackers, mixed for mood wheel

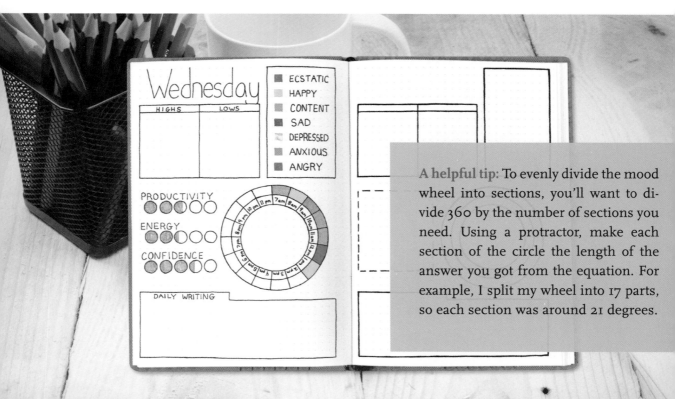

A helpful tip: To evenly divide the mood wheel into sections, you'll want to divide 360 by the number of sections you need. Using a protractor, make each section of the circle the length of the answer you got from the equation. For example, I split my wheel into 17 parts, so each section was around 21 degrees.

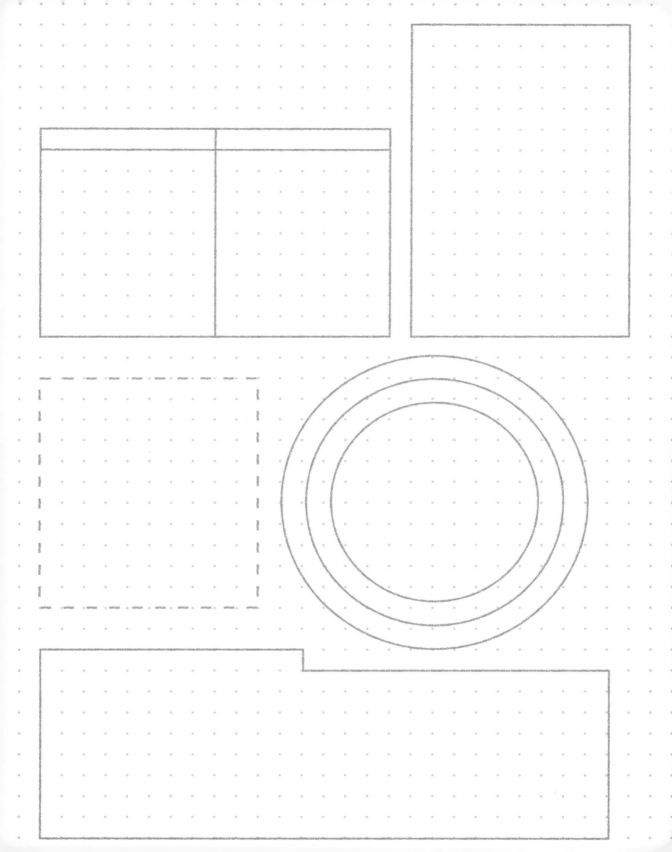

DAILY SPREAD 5: HORIZONTAL PAGE

I'm always so impressed by how simple changes can revolutionize a layout. In this case, all it took was turning my journal on its side. Suddenly, there was so much space to craft a creative page for my daily. This design features a variety of different-sized boxes shooting out from a center circle that marks the day of the week. It's perfect if you're looking for: a) a challenge, b) a customizable layout, or c) a spread that makes people go, "How did you do that?????" every time you show it off.

What you need: A pencil, a ruler, a 1-$^7/_8$-inch (25 mm) circular stencil
Color scheme: Black (seriously, I love the minimalist color scheme paired with the experimental spread)

A helpful tip: Don't worry too much about making your boxes the same size as mine! I actually made mine random sizes before assigning titles. Think about how much space you need for the things you want to track, and move forward from there.

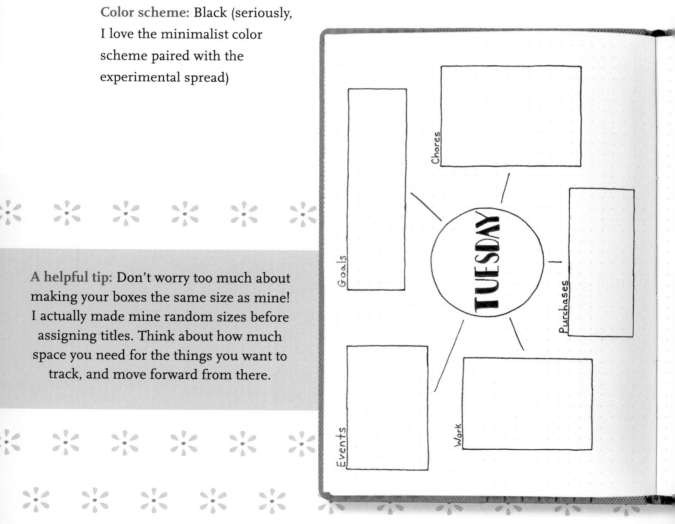

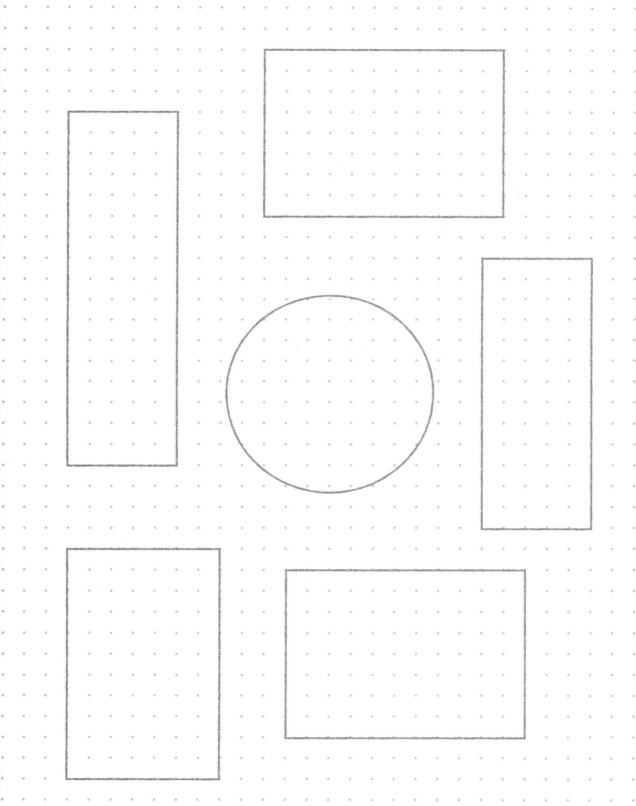

TRACKERS

Ah, trackers—the lifeblood of the dot journal! The powerhouse of the cell! The . . . sauce to pasta? Anyway, the point stands. Trackers truly invigorate the dot journal, and that's because they tend to be not only efficient, but also eye-catching, even at their most minimalist. A tracker will basically monitor a set of habits/chores/tasks along a similar theme, so you can stay focused and get things done over a set length of time (think the course of a day, week, month, or year). Believe me, nothing embarrasses me into shape more than seeing an empty tracker at the end of the month with chores like "Make Bed."

Daily vs. Weekly vs. Monthly Trackers

A question that a lot of people ask (and I often ask myself) is which duration tracker is most effective. After all, any tracker you make can be modified to fit a daily, weekly, monthly, even yearly spread. So how do you know which is best? To answer that, take a look inside your dot journal. What spreads do you find yourself using the most? That's where you'll want to place most of your trackers.

Personally, I tend to focus on the big picture, so I check my Monthly Spread most often. Because of this, I like to make monthly trackers of everything I want to monitor. This works really well for me as I'm not necessarily making spreads or spending a lot of time writing in my dot journal each day. However, if you find yourself with a lot of weekly or daily habits you want to keep aware of, a shorter tracker that you make more often is probably a better fit.

This brings up another issue: time. The monthly or yearly tracker will by nature be less time consuming, as a daily tracker you will have to make over and over again. This isn't necessarily a bad thing—the benefit of a daily or weekly tracker is that you can change it depending on your needs. If one week you need to track your water intake because there's a heat wave, and the next you need to track your sleep because you have early mornings at work, then the flexibility of a shorter tracker can be hugely beneficial.

None of this means you must commit to one style of tracker over the other! Many people, myself included, use a mix of both. For example, I use a yearly tracker for my finances, a monthly tracker for my mood, and a weekly tracker for chores. It's all about finding a balance of what works best for you.

TRACKER SPREAD 1: YEARLY BUDGET

No need to fear late fees with this helpful tracker! The budget tracker monitors bills for the entire year, so you can know the amount you owe and the date you paid it. This is a single page tracker, split into six sections over 12 months for all recurring utilities. This layout is excellent for those who want a long-term means of recording their budget, or anyone who doesn't want to devote a new page each month to their bills.

What you need: A pencil, a ruler
Color scheme: Black for outline and text, light green for subtitle filler, dark green for header

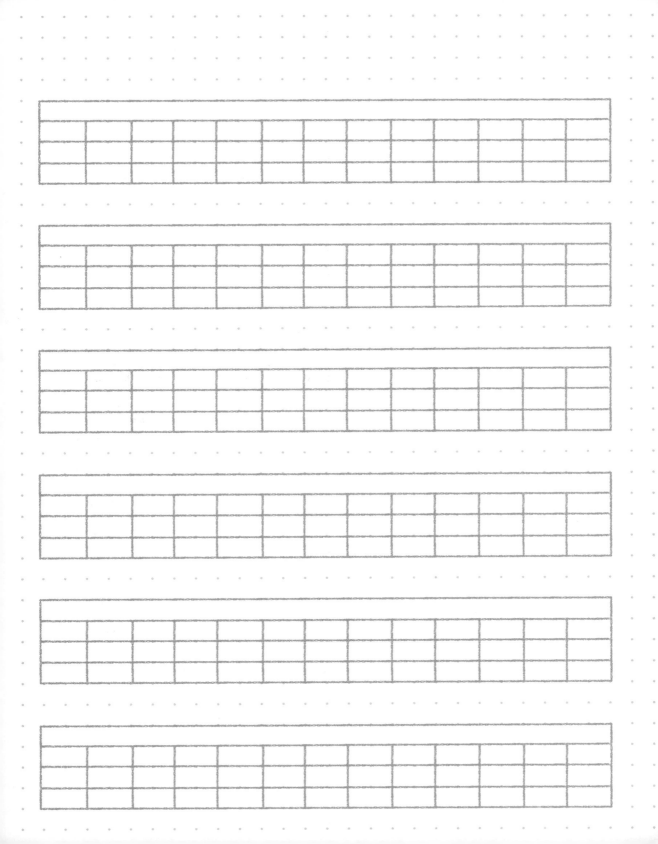

TRACKER SPREAD 2: YEARLY MOOD TRACKER

You'll find lots of mood trackers for every spread, but this one is a personal favorite, thanks to its look and space efficiency. It only takes up one page for the whole year, but ends up being one of the most colorful pages in a dot journal. This tracker is made up of a grid split into 12 months, which can be filled in according to mood. The key on the side makes it easy to understand, so at the end of the year you can look back and see a map of your feelings that looks almost like pixels on an old-school video game.

What you need: A pencil, a ruler
Color scheme: Black for outline and text, any colors for everything else

A helpful tip: Don't worry about tracing your grid in pen after the pencil work is done. The look is much cleaner, and the process is easier when you skip the pen and just start coloring! By the end, you should have a page of uninterrupted color!

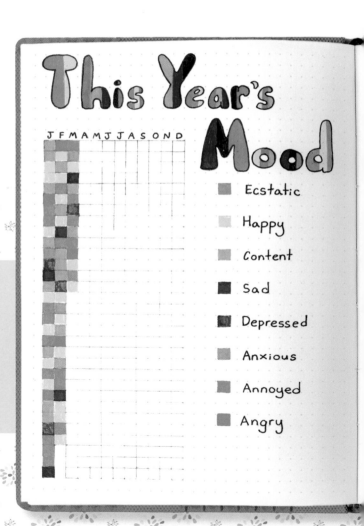

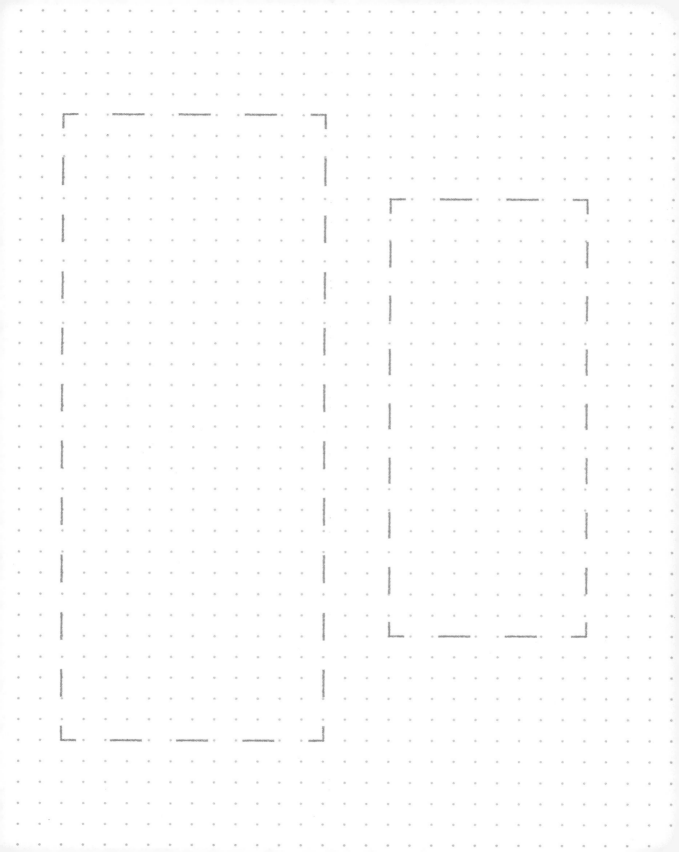

TRACKER SPREAD 3: REUSABLE PACKING LIST

It's a little more of a checklist than a traditional tracker, but it's so immensely helpful it deserves to be in this category. This tracker allows you to mark items as you pack, without making it seem like you need to pack everything on the list, as each trip comes with its own packing needs. This tracker is split into four sections (which can be modified as needed), and along the top features a place for you to note the date and location of your next trip out of town. Use this and never forget your toothbrush again!

What you need: A pencil, a ruler
Color scheme: Gray for outline and title, black for text, mixed colors for section fillers (purple, yellow, blue, pink)

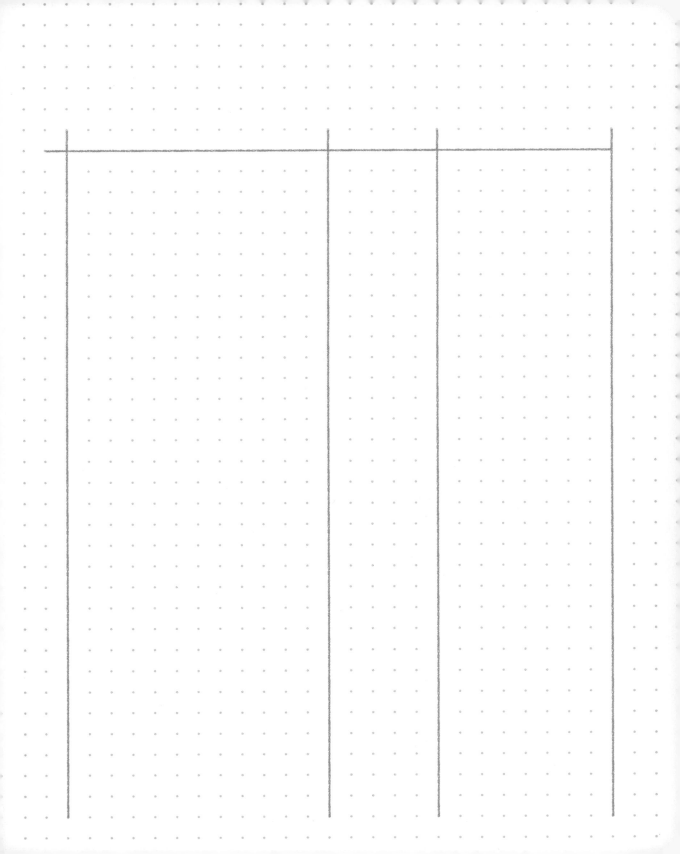

TRACKER SPREAD 5: CIRCULAR WELLNESS TRACKER

Remember what I said in the last chapter about turning your journal on its side? Well, that's precisely what happens again for this Wellness Tracker! Now, you can use this for any theme you'd like, but I found wellness to fit this layout very well, as it can be easily split into two mini trackers for physical and mental health. On a single page, each tracker allows for three habits to be monitored, with room along the inside for dates. This layout is also very forgiving, so if you find you can't make the circles as neat as you'd like, a thick pen can easily be incorporated for a mod look.

What you need: A pencil, a ruler, four stencils: 2-¾" (70 mm), 2-¼" (57 mm), 1-¾" (45 mm), 1-¼" (32 mm)

Color scheme: Black for title and outline, mixed colors for each week

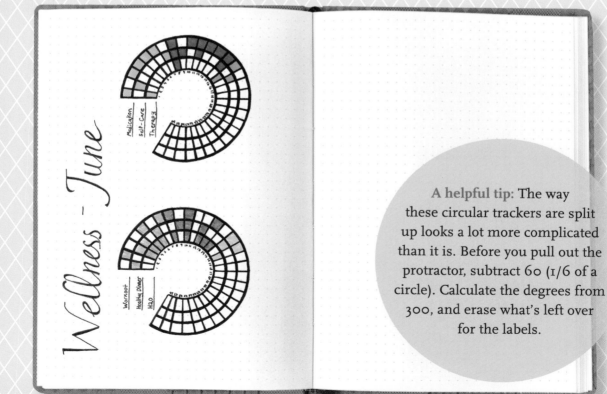

A helpful tip: The way these circular trackers are split up looks a lot more complicated than it is. Before you pull out the protractor, subtract 60 (1/6 of a circle). Calculate the degrees from 300, and erase what's left over for the labels.

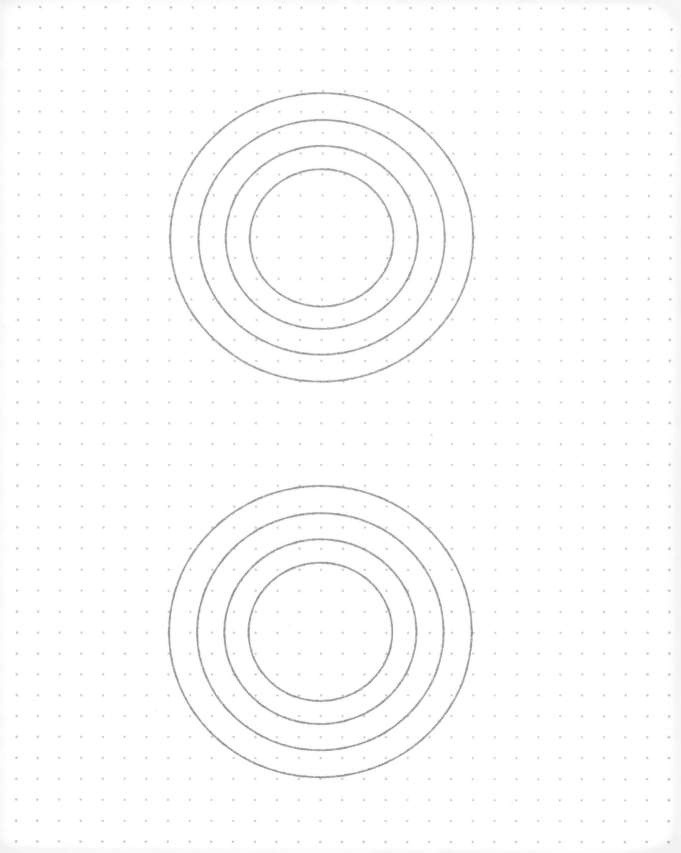

TRACKER SPREAD 6: ULTIMATE CHORES TRACKER

As I've hinted at many times in this book, I'm not the best roommate, which is a nice way of saying I never do the dishes. Luckily, trackers for chores can be very helpful, as they serve as unforgiving reminders when you forget to do something as basic as taking out the trash. This tracker is helpful for everyone (yes, even you) because it covers everything. The page is turned horizontally, leaving room for 20 chores to be monitored over the course of a month. Even if some of them, like checking the air filter, only get done once, this layout makes sure that they happen.

What you need: A pencil, a ruler
Color scheme: Black for outline and text, black for title, shades of blue for header, mixed colors for each day

A helpful tip: Much like the yearly mood tracker, don't worry about outlining the entire grid! It's just as clean, and easier, if you leave it blank until you fill that day in.

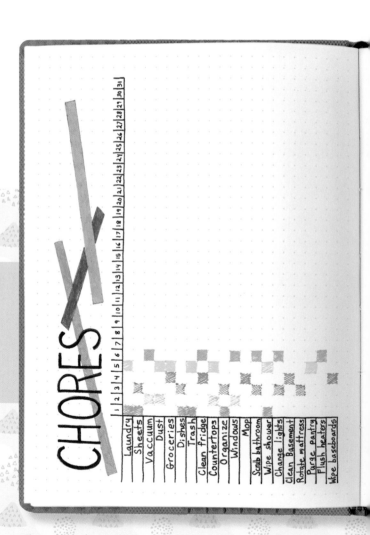

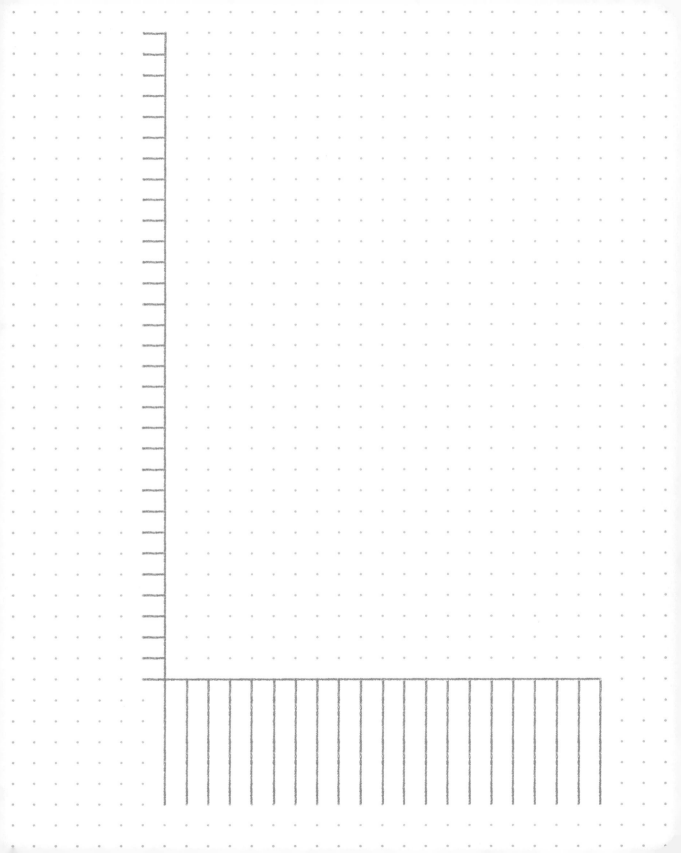

LISTS

I always find that lists are one of the more laid-back aspect of dot journaling, because they aren't restricted by time. You may have to design a new spread for each upcoming month, but lists can be added in whenever you feel you have the time.

Lists can be used for anything in, well, list form.

1. Christmas shopping? Make a list.
2. Movies you want to watch? Make a list.
3. Funny podcast titles? Make a list.

See how easy it is? Try not to get bogged down with ideas of what deserves to be in your dot journal, and just put in whatever you find interesting. I once had a list in my dot journal titled "Ghost Sounds," where I wrote down every new ghost sound I heard in horror movies. Lists reinforce the fact that dot journals are individual projects—no two will look the same or feature the same content, and that's a good thing.

Where Should I Put My Lists?

You can put your lists anywhere! Some are time specific, like if you're making a shopping list for the month, but many are ongoing, and can simply be placed in your dot journal whenever they come to mind. If you make a "Books to Read" list in January, that's the same list you'll be returning to in April. Just do what feels natural!

Design Elements

Sometimes, when you look through dot journals, it can feel like every single spread needs to be highly detailed and artistic, but this isn't the case, and that's especially true with lists! I mean, it's in the name. For any of the lists I show you in this chapter, it's super easy to just make a bulleted list and get the same result. Big layouts are a great option if you have the time and if it's something you're interested in, but they're not necessary, and your dot journal can still be very successful without them.

LIST SPREAD 1: MEAL PLAN/SHOPPING LIST

This spread not only helps you avoid going to the grocery store twice, but also helps you plan your meals! If you're anything like me, meal planning often consists of panicking right before the weekly shopping trip, followed by reheating leftovers. This list gives you tons of space to map out what meals you're going to cook, and exactly what you need to purchase to cook them. The best part? Each box is perfectly spaced for the average sticky note. This means that the Meal Plan/Shopping List is totally reusable. No need to create this spread over and over again each week—simply stick in a new note and get planning!

What you need: A pencil, a ruler, sticky notes
Optional: Washi tape for flair
Color scheme: Black for outline, blue for meal plan title, pink for groceries title, green and blue sticky notes
List ideas like this: Weekly Outfit Planning / General Shopping List

MEAL PLAN

TUE
Stuffed Peppers

THU
Pasta w/meatballs

Garlic Bread

SAT
Chicken Parm

ream

GROCERIES

VEGGIES
- Bell Peppers
- Cauliflower
- Broccoli
- Carrots

REFRIGERATED
- milk
- heavy cream
- yogurt
- Jello

FRUITS
- Kiwis
- white Peaches

CANNED
- tomatoes
- Baby corn

FROZEN
- Pizza
- veggie mix
- shredded coconut
- ice Pops

MISC
- trash bags
- Paper towels

LIST SPREAD 2: DREAM HOME

Real estate agents and leasing offices are very skilled at making you forget what you actually care about when viewing a potential home. If someone shows me a full bathtub, I'll forget that there is no washer/dryer. Never be distracted again with the apartment spread! This list is divided into three sections so you can focus on what you Need, Want, and Like, so you can make sure the next place you live checks all the boxes and then some.

What you need: A pencil, a ruler
Color scheme: Black for outline and text, pink and green for title
List ideas like this: College Scouting / Dream Job Requirements / Car Shopping

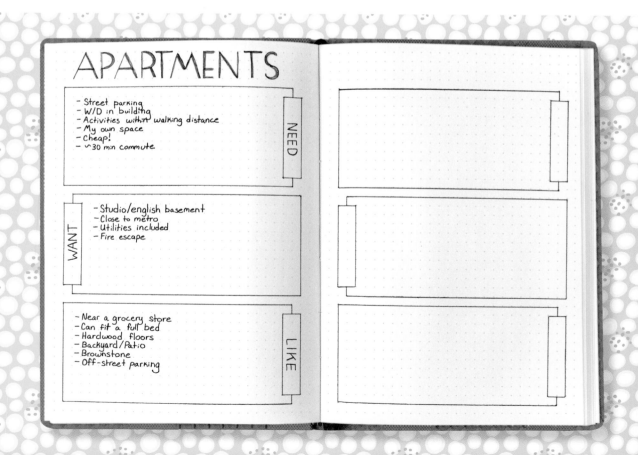

LIST SPREAD 3: THINGS TO DO IN ...

This list is loosely based on a spread I made for my partner when they moved out of state for a new job. It was super useful in both helping them acclimate to their new city, and in giving us things to do together. The page is split in half, with the top half featuring an outline of the state with a few landmarks, and the bottom half organizing activities and sights based on location. This spread isn't just great for new places though—I've done this with my home state and found lots of new places to visit and things to do that I'd just never thought to research.

What you need: A pencil, a ruler
Color scheme: Black for outline, text, and title, red colored pencil for state fill-in
List ideas like this:
Travel Destinations /
Foodie Chart / Date Ideas

A helpful tip: There are many stencil packs available in the shapes of the different states. You might also try drawing the map of a city or area if you are focusing on a very specific area.

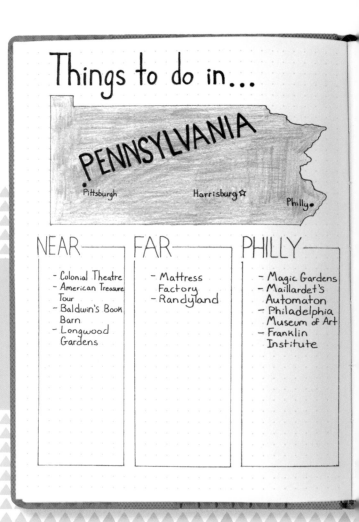

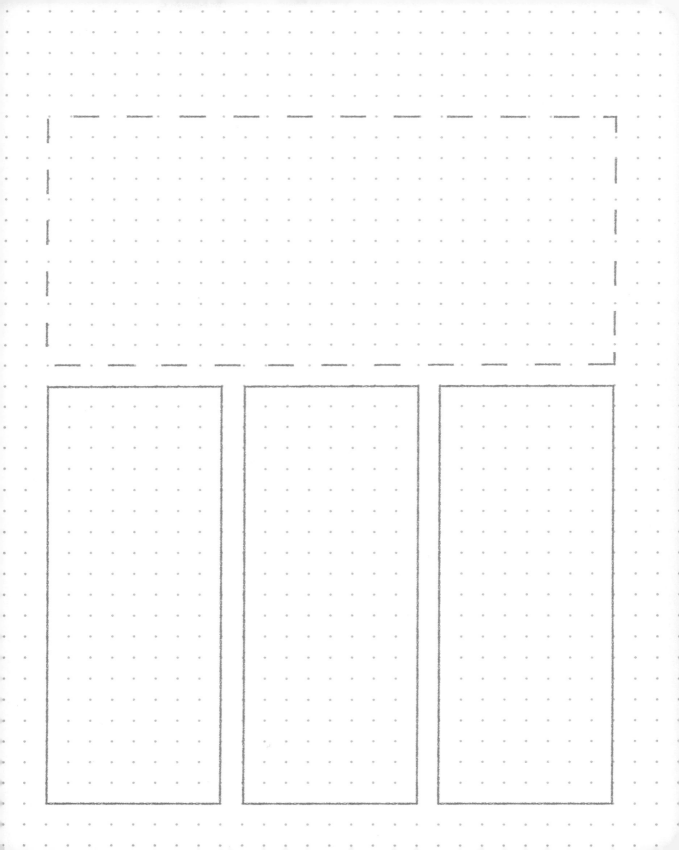

LIST SPREAD 4: GRATITUDES

Gratitudes really are the heart of dot journals, and there are almost infinite ways to do them. Some people like to just leave a little room in their monthly or weekly spreads to incorporate them, and others like to devote whole pages to their gratitudes. How you choose to organize what you're thankful for is up to you, but I think this design is lovely, and simpler than it looks, especially since by this point in the book, you've had a lot of practice with circular stencils. This design features an array of 30 sunbeams for the month, with room in each to quickly jot down something great from the day. This mix of colors reinforces the message: There's something bright everywhere.

What you need: A pencil, a ruler, a 2-¾" (70 mm) stencil, a protractor
Color scheme: Black for outline, text, and title, mixed colored pencils for sunbeams
List ideas like this: Daily Observations / Prayers / Well Wishes

A helpful tip: Since this design only uses half of a circular stencil, when you section off the sunbeams, make sure you're dividing from 180 instead of 360 before pulling out the protractor.

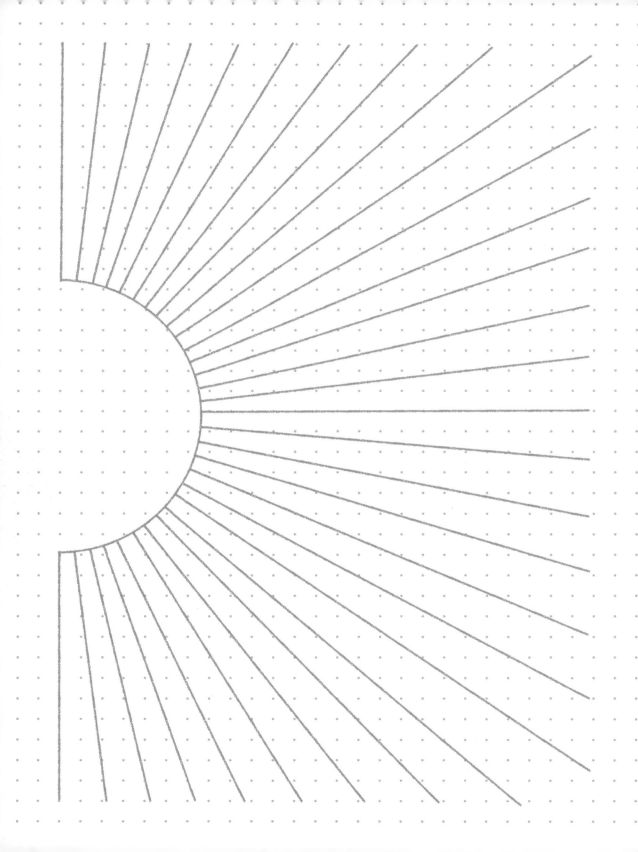

LIST SPREAD 5: MOVIE WATCH LIST

People are always giving me recommendations for movies that I never get around to seeing, mostly because I forget to write them down. The Movie Watch List gives you lots of space to plan showings for the next year (or month, depending on how often you organize showings). This list is split into four sections for four genres, and is designed to look like movie reels, so everyone is sure to know how much you know about film. There's room in each box for as much info as you see fit: for some, that might just be the title and the year, for others, that may include actors and a brief(!) synopsis.

What you need: A pencil, a ruler
Color scheme: Black for outline, title, and text
List ideas like this: Books to Read / Television Shows to Watch

LIST SPREAD 6: PLAYLIST

When the one song you've been playing on repeat suddenly isn't doing it any-more, a good playlist is crucial. While Spotify will make you a new one each month, there's a lot to be said for face-to-face recommendations. Like the Mov-ie Watch List, the Playlist allows you to mark all the songs and albums your friends have been telling you to listen to. This spread features drawings of multi-colored iPods, each with room for both the album (or song) title and the artist's name, so you know what you can listen to the next time your favorite band breaks up.

What you need: A pencil, a ruler
Color scheme: Black for outline and text, mixed colored pencils for iPod fillers
List ideas like this:
Concerts of the Month / Style Icons

A helpful tip: I chose to simply fill in the iPods with some bright colors, and write in the album titles and artists, but if you want to go the extra mile, you can print out the album covers and cut them to size to fit in your spread.

MISTAKES

By this point in your dot journaling process, it's possible that you've encountered a couple of slip-ups. Sometimes you're working in a café, and someone bumps into your table. Sometimes you make incorrect measurements. Sometimes, a spread you thought would be simple turns out to be really complicated. It's okay, these things happen, and I promise, they're not the end of the world.

Believe me, I know. In the process of writing this book, I've made more mistakes than I can count. Luckily, this experience has given me some life-saving info I can now pass onto you, so no smudged pen or torn page seems too dire.

Avoiding Mistakes

Now, I know, this chapter is supposed to help you deal with existing mistakes, but to cover all our bases, it's important to do everything to avoid them. Not all mistakes can be dodged, but there are a few tips I've discovered that can help prevent them from being a too common occurrence.

Start in pencil. Yes, I know what you're thinking: "Hannah, I'm already doing this! You've said it a million times!" But here's the thing, the longer you dot journal, the more you're going to be tempted to not use a pencil. Maybe it's your fourth time doing the same spread, and you're convinced you can do it with your eyes closed. Don't fall for this trap! It's a devil on your shoulder! Avoid my heartbreak. Pencil first.

Use a ruler and/or stencil. I'm firmly of the belief that our hands weren't made to draw straight lines. Using a ruler and a stencil will ensure that shaking hands never get the better of you. I even like to push a little into the ruler as I draw for the extra security.

Plan ahead. This involves two key steps. The first is knowing the dimensions of your page (how many blocks horizontally? How many vertically? Where is the midpoint?). The second step is finding designs that you like, and counting the dimensions to make sure they'll fit in your dot journal. No two dot journals are the same, so you want to make sure that you can alter the spread to work for you!

Give yourself room! Giving yourself room means asking the question, "How do I best organize the page for what I actually need?" as opposed to just making the design you think will look cool. Sometimes I get so concerned with making sure that the boxes are proportional, without even considering the fact that my notes can't fit into four split boxes across the bottom half of the page. Think about how big your handwriting is, how many tasks you have a day, and how much space you want for your notes and observations.

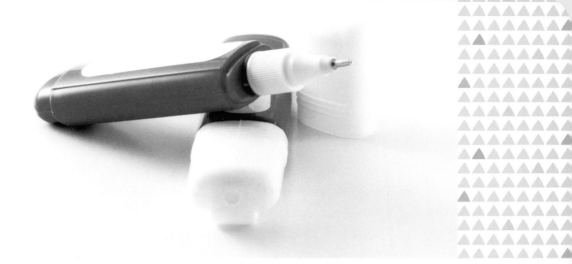

White-Out

Ah, white-out: Wite-Out, Liquid Paper, correction fluid, correction tape, correction pen . . . Using your correction method of choice is like being back in grade school. Never underestimate their effectiveness—many mistakes can be forgotten with a quick swipe of white. However, different types are better fitted to different situations.

Fluid. Fluid is an excellent option for covering up mistakes, especially if you need to cover large swaths of space, or if you accidentally got marker on an area that's supposed to be blank. As long as you give it time to dry, you'll get great coverage. However, I wouldn't recommend using fluid on a part of the page where you intend to write or draw, as ink/marker can't sink into it the same way they sink into paper.

Tape. Correction tape is much more effective if you'd like to write on top of it, and its design makes it easy to cover smaller areas. I've had a lot of success using it over uneven lines, and it works so well I genuinely can't notice it when I'm done. However, this won't work so well on super small areas, so don't expect to be able to fix a single letter—you'll have to rewrite the whole word.

Pen (white gel). If you're committed to fixing the smallest of mistakes, white gel pen is the answer. It can easily cover tiny spots or stains. It's not meant for writing over, but if you want to fix the width of a letter, then having this on hand will save you lots of strife.

Washi Tape and Stickers

Sometimes, things just can't be erased. That's where washi tape and stickers come in. They're not just for decorative flair, they're also extremely helpful in hiding any embarrassing marks on the page. Sometimes, though, and it's important to say, you have to kill your darlings. If a box is beyond repair, cover the whole thing in washi tape—make it decorative! You'll have less room to write, but the page will be gorgeous.

A helpful tip: On the opposite page, I've taken a weekly spread that would normally have a tracker on the bottom right of the page and covered it in dark washi tape. To further hide my mistake/make the page look intentional, I've also placed a strip of the same washi tape next to the title. I find it helpful to make moves like this throughout my dot journal spreads. When a sense of symmetry is created, the whole page looks much more deliberate.

WEEK 1

MONDAY

TUESDAY

WEDNESDAY

THURSDAY

FRIDAY

SATURDAY

SUNDAY

Adding a Blank Page

This technique looks so good, I'm often tempted to use it even when I don't have a mistake to cover up! All it takes is some thick card stock (either in white to match the page, or any fun color for added flair) and some tape. Cut the paper to fit the dimensions of the page, paste, and draw on top of it.

A word to the wise: Since this card stock likely won't have a dotted grid, you can't exactly re-create a measured spread. However, you can create a successful design page that introduces a month's spread or tracker or list!

For the cover-up on the right, I've layered a couple of pages of card stock on top of one another before using a large circular stencil to make a visual for August. I liked the effect of the pages almost popping out of the journal, but if you're looking to make something more subtle, I would recommend using glue to make sure everything is as securely attached as possible.

Cross It Out

I love crossing things out. I love crossing out sentences that don't make any sense, I love crossing out bad doodles in my notebook, and I especially love crossing out bad spreads in my dot journal. Crossing things out is not only allowed, it's encouraged. Sometimes, a page is beyond saving, and it just isn't worth it to put in even more time trying to cover it up. Unless you're writing a book on how to dot journal (😊), it's totally fine to leave behind proof of your humanity. Do it for me.

DESIGN ELEMENTS

Congratulations, you've made it to the last chapter of this book, which means you've got a real grasp on dot journaling, and have (hopefully) been making spreads and lists that help organize your day-to-day life. Again, congratulations! It's hard work, but the result is a planner/art project/scrapbook/diary/movie watch list completely and totally tailored to you. Not a lot of people can make that happen.

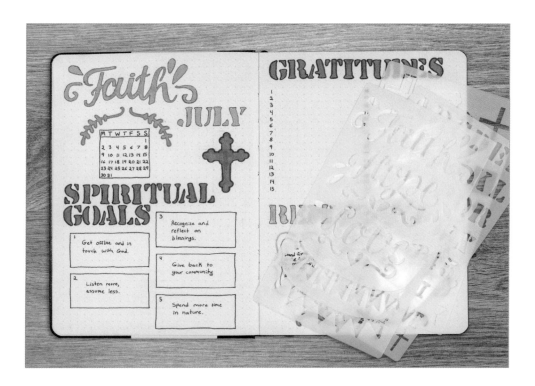

Maybe by this point, you're a real pro. You wanna go even further. You wanna make the kinds of spreads that you only see on Instagram, or craftfully edited YouTube videos. I get it. Here's the good news. It's not as hard as you think. If you incorporate just a few techniques, you too can have the kind of dot journal people see and go green with envy. "Yes, Karen," you will say with pride, "I did make this myself."

Color and Color Theory

The easiest way to elevate a spread is incorporating a bit of color, but this can become a bit tricky as not all colors complement each other. So here are some quick tips on what colors best go together so you know what you can put on the page for that extra bit of flair.

Let's take a look at this color wheel. Using this as a base, it's very easy to find color combinations that work 100 percent of the time. That's right, no guess-work required. You have:

Complementary. Pick a color on the wheel, then find the color right across from it. That's your complementary color combo. So, if we look at green on the color wheel, its complementary color would be red. This is a great strategy for picking a color scheme when you only need two colors.

Triad. To find a triad all you have to do is make an equilateral triangle on the wheel. If you're having difficulty finding one, the best place to start is with the primary colors: yellow, blue, and red. These make a perfect triangle, so you know all of the colors will go together. From that point, you can simply rotate that triangle around the wheel to find new combinations.

Analogous. The analogous scheme is made up of two to five colors that are next to one another. So, if we look at yellow, its analogous colors would be orange, green, and blue. I find that this scheme works best when muted or pastel colors are used, so as not to overwhelm the eye.

Square. Similar to the triad, all you need to do to make this scheme is place a square on the wheel. If you look, you will notice that the top left and bottom right corners (and by extension the top right and bottom left corners) of the square are complementary colors, and the top and bottom corners are analogous, making this combination the best of both worlds.

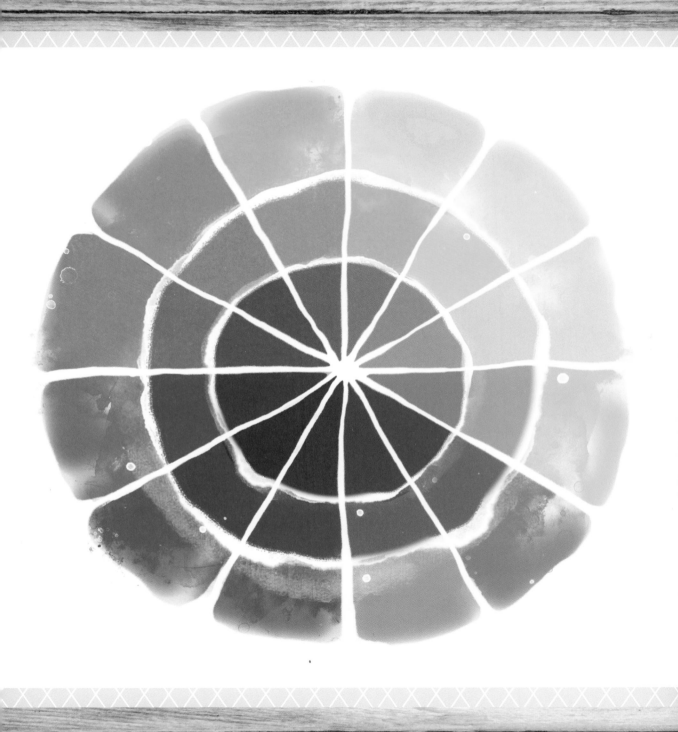

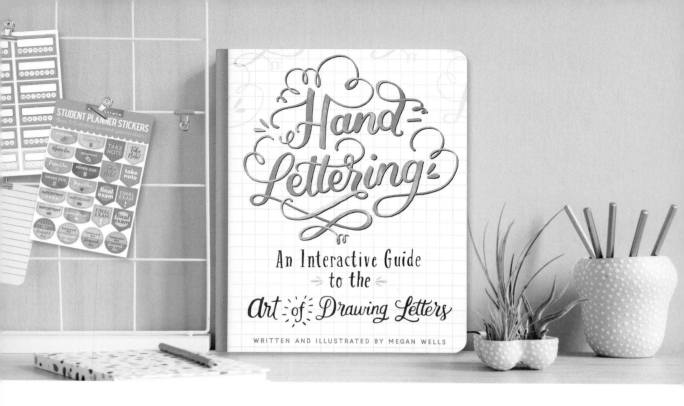

Titles and Lettering

It's definitely not the easiest, but one of the most effective ways of bringing that extra edge to your dot journaling is to write in a variety of fonts. Not the whole page (oh my gosh—can you imagine??), but titles, headers, and quotes, are great spots to spend a little time on your lettering. There are two ways you can go about this:

Copy Existing Fonts. I, personally, the laziest person on Earth, vouch wholeheartedly for this method. All you do is type what you want into a word processing document, pick the font you like, and then copy it! This is a great way to title your work because your phrase is laid out for you so you don't have to worry at all about sizing. However, make sure to give yourself lots of time to sketch out the letters before committing to ink.

Learn Hand Lettering. This is perhaps harder in the short term, but once mastered, it will make titles a breeze! (There are several good books on this topic; one excellent resource is *Hand-Lettering: An Interactive Guide to the Art of*

Drawing Letters, by Megan Wells, www.makewells.com.) Part of why I love this book is that the author not only shows you step by step how to draw each font, but she also gives you ample room to practice!

Section Breaks

Section breaks are one of the easiest ways to split up a page. This is especially useful if you're making a spread that will incorporate a lot of white space. It's an easy way to fill up an otherwise sparse spread, while also still doing functional work.

One option for section breaks is washi tape, which is easy, colorful, and quick to come by at almost any craft store. However, you can also draw section breaks by incorporating designs like vines, banners, and small doodles (think stars, moons, flowers, etc.).

However, drawing each section break can be a pain, especially since when you draw freehand, it's harder to make things even. That's why I recommend using stencils for these, to make a quick and easy addition to your dot journaling. Peter Pauper Press makes a great Dot Journal stencil set.

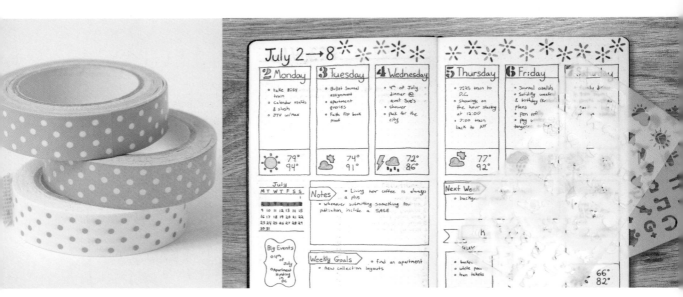

Turning Spreads into Art: Alexander Calder

If you find you have a lot of time and want to make a spread that is not only functional, but also a piece of art, one of the best things you can do is look up an artist you admire, and make some designs inspired from their work. They might not be the most efficient spreads (as in order to incorporate the art, some sections might be smaller than others), but they will be stunning. Plus, it's a great way to incorporate your passions not just into the substance of your journal, but also the bones of it.

I have always loved the artist Alexander Calder (1898–1976, calder.org), known for his abstract art. Photos of two of his sculptures, *The Halberdier*, left, and *Crinkly with Red Disc*, right, are below. His work is whimsical, and plays with balance in a way that makes me nervous (in a good way, of course!). I wanted to see if I could replicate that in some of my own designs, so I created Monthly and Weekly Spreads inspired by his work, as well as a Sleep Tracker.

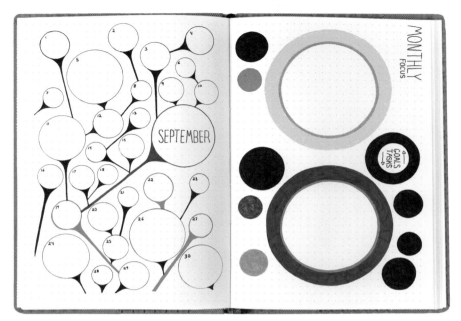

Monthly Spread, Dates – Based on *Fleches*, 1968 lithograph, from a Calder exhibition at Galerie Maeght in Paris, lithograph in color. / **Monthly Focus, Goals and Tasks** – Based on *6 Cercles*, 1973, tempera on paper.

Weekly Log – Based on *Composition*, circa 1967, lithograph, and *Balloons*, 1970, print.
Sleep Tracker – Based on *Pyramids and Spirals*, 1974, lithograph in color.

• Practice Pages •

ABOUT THE AUTHOR:

Hannah Beilenson is a freelance writer, poet, student, teacher, and a devoted dot journaler. She's also on the lookout for the next best sandwich.

SUPPLIES AVAILABLE FROM PETER PAUPER PRESS:

Essentials Dot Matrix Notebooks. Visit www.peterpauper.com for a variety of dot matrix notebooks.

Studio Series Micro-Line Pens provide controlled, consistent, smooth fluid lines for drawing, writing, illustration, and dot journaling!

Studio Series Color Micro-Line Pen Set. Micro-pigmented inks create fine, consistent, fluid lines. Includes pens in black, red, blue, green, purple, brown, and yellow.

Studio Series Fine-Line Marker Set. Journal, draw, and write in 30 different colors with this artist's quality marker set.

Studio Series Watercolor Brush Pens. Create gorgeous watercolor effects with this bristle brush pen set. Vivid colors blend beautifully, by themselves or with water from the included water brush. 24 colors. 1 water brush for blending.

Visit us at www.peterpauper.com

Photo Credits p. 138: **Left** – Wikimedia Commons contributors, "File: Hannover Calder Modern art.jpg," Wikimedia Commons, the free media repository, https://bit.ly/2pPvu2s (accessed October 16, 2019).
Right – Wikimedia Commons contributors, "File: Alexander Calder Crinkly avec disc Rouge 1973-1.jpg," Wikimedia Commons, the free media repository, https://bit.ly/34c79TB (accessed October 16, 2019).